Transportation Around the World

Trucks

Chris Oxlade

Heinemann Library
Chicago, Illinois

©2001, 2008 Heinemann Library
a division of Reed Elsevier Inc.
Chicago, Illinois

Customer Service 888-454-2279
Visit our website at www.heinemannraintree.com

Designed by Kimberly R. Miracle, Ray Hendren, Cavedweller Studio and Q2A Creative
Printed in China by WKT

12 11 10 09 08
10 9 8 7 6 5 4 3 2 1

New edition ISBN-10:   1-4329-0205-9 (hardcover)
                         1-4329-0214-8 (paperback)
New edition ISBN-13:   978-1-4329-0205-6 (hardcover)
                         978-1-4329-0214-8 (paperback)

The Library of Congress has cataloged the first edition as follows:
Oxlade, Chris.
        Trains / Chris Oxlade.
                    p. cm. — (Transportation around the world)
        Includes bibliographical references (p.   ) and index.
ISBN 1-57572-307-7 (library binding)
1.   Railroads — Trains — Juvenile literature.
        [1. Railroads - Trains.] I. Title. II. Series.

TF148 .O95 2001
625.1 — dc21

                                                          00-010065

Acknowledgements
The publishers would like to thank the following for permission to reproduce photographs: R.D. Battersby pp. **15**, **26**; Trevor Clifford p. **10**; Corbis p. **22**; Eye Ubiquitous pp. **9**, **11**, **13**, **14**, **16**, **29**; David Hoffman p. **23**; Masterfile pp. **4** (Ken Davies), **24** (Snowplow); Peter Sawell & Partners/Freight Transport Association p. **6**; Pictures p. **27**; Quadrant pp. **7**, **12**, **17**, **18**, **19**, **28**; Science and Society Picture Library p. **8**; Tony Stone Images pp. **20**, **25**; Travel Ink p. **5** (Tony Page); John Walmsley p. **21**.

Cover photograph reproduced with permission of Corbis (Ken Davies).

Every effort has been made to contact copyright holders of any material reproduced in this book. Any omissions will be rectified in subsequent printings if notice is given to the publisher.

Contents

Some words are shown in bold, **like this**. You can find out what they mean by looking in the glossary.

What Is a Truck?

A truck is a large vehicle that moves along on wheels. Trucks carry goods called **cargo**. At the front of the truck is a **cab** where the driver sits. At the back is a big space for the cargo.

Tanker trucks like this carry liquid cargo.

This truck is carrying glass bottles in crates to the grocery store.

Cargo is loaded onto trucks. The trucks carry the heavy cargo to where it is needed. Then the cargo is unloaded again.

How Trucks Work

A truck mechanic, like this man, is an expert at fixing engines.

A truck has an **engine** that makes its wheels turn, moving it along. The engine needs to be powerful to move the heavy **cargo**. It needs **fuel** to make it work.

Truck wheels are usually larger than those of a car, to carry the heavy cargo.

Trucks have wheels that go around. Each wheel has a **rubber tire** around it. Small trucks have four wheels. Some big trucks have twelve wheels or even more.

Old Trucks

The first trucks using **engines** were built almost 100 years ago. The engines were **steam** engines, like the ones used in steam trains. Before engines, horses and wagons transported **cargo**.

Trucks with steam engines moved more slowly than modern trucks.

Pickup trucks were first built in the 1930s. They had gasoline engines instead of steam engines. Today many people drive modern pickup trucks.

This is one of the early pickup trucks used in the United States.

Where Trucks Are Used

Big trucks carry **cargo** along main roads. They travel between towns and cities. The smooth, hard road surface allows the trucks to travel quickly.

Big trucks like this one were made to carry cargo for long distances.

Some trucks go through areas where there are no roads, or just dirt tracks. The ground can get very muddy. The drivers must know how to drive safely over rough ground.

Trucks have large, sturdy wheels to keep the driver and the cargo safe on dirt roads.

11

Flatbed Trucks

This type of truck is useful for carrying cargo that would not fit into other trucks.

A truck with a flat **cargo** space is called a flatbed truck. It can carry almost any kind of cargo. The cargo is tied in place to stop it from falling off.

crane

The crane does the heavy lifting for the driver.

This flatbed truck has its own mini **crane** behind the **cab**. The crane lifts cargo onto and off of the truck. The driver moves **levers** to work the crane.

Articulated Trucks

An articulated truck bends in the middle. This makes it easier to go around corners. The part where the **cargo** is carried is called a trailer.

Articulated trucks are useful for carrying cargo long distances.

The front part with the driver's **cab** and **engine** is called the tractor unit. It pulls the trailer along. It can be moved from one trailer and attached to another.

This man is attaching the trailer to his tractor unit.

cab

trailer

Road Trains

A road train is an articulated truck with two or three trailers instead of just one. Road trains can often be seen in Australia, carrying **cargo** and farm animals.

Road trains have very powerful **engines** to pull heavy cargo over long distances.

This is the inside of the cab, including the driver's sleeping area.

Long-distance trucks such as road trains often travel for several days. Inside the **cab** is a bed where the driver sleeps at night. Some trucks also have cabinets for the driver's clothes.

Tanker Trucks

A tanker truck is a truck with a huge **tank** to carry **cargo**. Some tanks can be filled with liquids such as gasoline. Other tanks carry foods such as flour, grain, or beans.

Some tanker trucks, like this one, have more than one trailer.

valve

This tanker is unloading
its cargo.

The tank is filled up through holes in the top. After the
journey, the tank empties out through pipes at the
back. The driver opens **valves** to let the cargo out.

Dump Trucks

Monster dump trucks can carry tons of dirt, gravel, or rock.

A monster dump truck can be as tall as a house. The huge wheels are as tall as the truck driver. Monster dump trucks do not usually drive on roads. They work at **quarries** or building sites.

hydraulic arm

The huge wheels and strong hydraulic arms help keep the truck stable while dumping its heavy cargo.

The back of a dump truck tips up to make its **cargo** slide out onto the ground. Powerful **hydraulic** arms use water pressure to push out and make the back tip.

Garbage Trucks

Many types of trucks do special jobs instead of carrying **cargo**. Some trucks go around the streets collecting garbage. Some of the garbage is taken to a dump.

Trucks like this one also collect garbage that will be recycled.

A machine lifts trash cans and shakes the garbage from them into the back of the truck. Inside the truck is another machine that crushes the garbage. This helps to pack more garbage into the truck.

This truck has a machine that picks up the trash can and dumps the garbage into the truck.

Snowplows

A snowplow is a special truck that clears ice and snow from roads. During the winter, snowplows keep roads open so that other vehicles can make their journeys safely.

At the front of the snowplow is a wide metal shovel called a plow. As the snowplow moves along, the plow pushes snow to the side of the road.

Snowplows must work in cold, dangerous conditions to help keep roads clear.

plow

Mobile Cranes

People can hire mobile **cranes** when they want heavy objects lifted. A mobile crane has sturdy wheels and **tires.** It can drive on roads or dirt tracks.

Trucks like this are often used at sites where building work is going on.

boom

hydraulic arm

A mobile crane uses a
hydraulic arm to make the
boom of the crane longer.

The crane has a boom that can reach high into
the air. The driver operates the crane from a **cab**.
Metal feet stop the crane from tipping over.

Monster Trucks

Monster trucks are amazing vehicles. Their owners make them from ordinary pickup trucks. They race against each other over bumpy tracks and obstacle courses.

Monster truck shows are very popular events in many countries.

Monster trucks have huge wheels. They have strong **suspensions** for landing after jumps. Inside the **cab** are strong bars that protect the driver if the truck rolls over.

A monster truck can be very scary, but very fun to watch.

Timeline

1769   Frenchman Nicholas Cugnot builds a truck to pull a huge gun. It is the first vehicle powered by a **steam engine**.

1830s   Steam-powered coaches are used in England to carry passengers between towns. They ruin the dirt roads.

1850s   Steam-powered traction engines are built to pull farm machinery. Similar trucks are used to pull wagons on the roads.

1892   German engineer Rudolph Diesel develops the diesel engine. Most large modern trucks have diesel engines.

1896   The first truck is built in Germany by Gottlieb Daimler. Trucks soon take the place of most horse-drawn wagons.

1940s   The first small four-wheel drive truck, called a Jeep, is built for the U.S. Army to use in World War II.

Glossary

cab   space at the front of a truck where the truck driver sits

cargo   goods that are moved from place to place

crane   machine for lifting large, heavy objects

engine   machine that uses fuel to power movement

fuel   substance that burns to make heat

hydraulic   moved by a liquid

lever   rod that tilts up and down or from side to side

quarry   place where rock is dug from the ground

rubber   soft, flexible material that is used to make tires

steam   water that has become a gas

suspension   system of springs that let a truck's wheels move up and down over bumps

tank   large container for storing something

tire   rubber ring that fits around the outside of a wheel. It is filled with air.

valve   device that opens and closes to let a liquid or a gas flow or stop it from flowing

Find Out More

Hubbell, Patricia. *Trucks: Whizz! Zoom! Rumble!* New York: Marshall Cavendish, 2003.

Simon, Seymour. *Seymour Simon's Book of Trucks.* New York: HarperTrophy, 2002.

Tiner, John Hudson. *Trucks.* Mankato, MN: Creative Education, 2003.

Index